Caribbean Rum Book

MACMILLAN CARIBBEAN

First published 1985

Published by *Macmillan Publishers Ltd*
London and Basingstoke
Associated companies and representatives in Accra,
Auckland, Delhi, Dublin, Gaborone, Hamburg, Harare,
Hong Kong, Kuala Lumpur, Lagos, Manzini, Melbourne,
Mexico City, Nairobi, New York, Singapore, Tokyo

ISBN 0 - 333 - 39800 - 9

Printed in Hong Kong

British Library Cataloguing in Publication Data
Caribbean rum book.
   1. Rum   2. Cocktails
   641.6'25   TX951
ISBN 0 333 39800 9

Acknowledgements

The publishers would like to thank the following
photographic sources for their help in supplying
photographs for this book.
J. Allan Cash (cover);
Anne Bolt and Maurice Yates;
Grants of St. James's;
Bill Lennox;
Media Relations Ltd.

Contents

The Story of Caribbean Rum

The tall grass in the waving fields, which is so much a feature of the Caribbean, is sugar cane. It is from the sugar cane crop that Caribbean rum is produced.

When the cane is ripe, or 'mature', it is cut and sent to the sugar factory. Cane has traditionally been cut by hand but now, increasingly, it is being cut by machine. The cut cane is sent to the sugar factory. In the sugar mill the juice is evaporated to a syrup and the sugar is made into crystals. Molasses is drained from the sugar in the curing house and finally it is taken to the distillery. Here the molasses is made into rum.

Molasses is mixed with water, fermented with yeast and then distilled. The distinctive flavour of each brand of rum is produced by the different types of molasses used, the method of distilling and the method and period of storage.

Rum is the Caribbean's own beverage. A precise date for the origination of rum is not known but it is estimated to be about 300 years ago during the Spanish colonisation of the West Indian islands. The Caribbean, at that time, was a hotbed of piracy. The pirates adopted rum as their drink and they then introduced it to Europe. Pirate vessels carried shipments of rum from the colonies to the Old World. After the First World War a new type of pirate emerged, the rum runner, who smuggled the spirit into the United States at the time of prohibition. Nowadays the North American visitor can carry his supplies of Caribbean rum legally back to his home.

Types of Rum

As is the case with all distilled spirits, rum is water-white when first distilled.

Amber and dark colouring rums obtain this colour from the extractives from the oak barrel during ageing and from caramel, a colouring agent which is sometimes used.

Light bodied rums are produced on sophisticated distillation units and have a light, delicate rum flavour. Among these are the white and amber-coloured rums of Trinidad, Puerto Rico, Cuba and the Virgin Islands.

Jamaica is famous for full-bodied, strong flavoured, dark rum.

From the Caribbean islands there are many varieties available with distinctive flavours so it is best to experiment until you find the one you like. The colouring of the dark Jamaican rum is produced naturally, either from burnt sugar or burnt molasses. The Demerara rum produced in Guyana has a more aromatic flavour.

Bar Equipment

Some of the basic equipment is illustrated here but a number of other items should be included with your bottle of rum.

The following check list is a useful starting point:
Bottle and can opener
Corkscrew
Ice bucket and tongs
Water jug (preferably one with a lip for retaining ice)
Mixing jug
Wooden chopping block and sharp knife – for cutting and preparing fruit
Squeezer for lemons and limes
Swizzle stick and muddler – for crushing ice and mint in the mixing jug or individual glass
A measure to ensure that the correct amount shown in the recipe is added.

The Glasses to Use

To properly appreciate your rum drink the most appropriate glass should be used. The examples illustrated below will be adequate for all varieties of rum recipes.

Measures

The equivalent measures for terms in the recipes are as follows:

1 dash	$\frac{1}{6}$ teaspoon
1 teaspoon	$\frac{1}{8}$ ounce
1 tablespoon	3 teaspoons
1 glass (wineglass)	4 ounces
1 cup	8 ounces

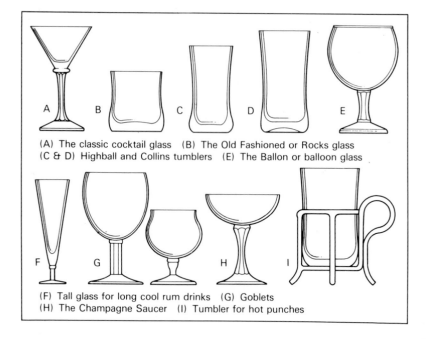

(A) The classic cocktail glass   (B) The Old Fashioned or Rocks glass
(C & D) Highball and Collins tumblers   (E) The Ballon or balloon glass

(F) Tall glass for long cool rum drinks   (G) Goblets
(H) The Champagne Saucer   (I) Tumbler for hot punches

Daiquiri

Daiquiri is a refreshing drink which often contains fruit. Usually white rum is used in a daiquiri, but this is not essential.

Daiquiri

Juice of half a lime
1 tsp sugar
1½ oz white rum
Shake with ice and strain into
a cocktail glass.

Banana Daiquiri

Juice of half a lime
1 tsp sugar
Chopped banana
1½ oz white rum
Shake and blend with ice.

Bee's kiss

1½ oz white rum
1 tbsp black coffee
1 tbsp fresh cream
Shake and blend with ice.

Frozen Daiquiri

In a blender place
6 oz white rum
1 tbsp fresh lime juice
2 tbsp sugar

either
½ a very ripe banana

or
⅓ cup tinned mango or
pineapple
2 cups ice

Blend until the final
consistency is like snow.

Passion Daiquiri

1½ oz white rum
1 tbsp passion fruit juice
Juice of 1 lime
1 tsp sugar
Shake with ice and strain into
a cocktail glass.

Cocktails

Rum forms the basis for many cooling cocktails. A few favourites are included here for you to shake and serve at almost any hour of the day or night.

Goombay Smash

1½ oz dark rum
¾ oz coconut rum
3 oz pineapple juice
¼ oz lemon juice
¼ oz Triple Sec
Dash of sugar syrup
Shake well and serve in a tall
glass with cracked ice, a
cherry and sliced lemon on
top of the glass.

Mai-Tai

2 oz rum
1 oz Curaçao
1 tbsp lime juice
1 tbsp Orgeat or
almond-flavoured syrup
1 tbsp Grenadine
½ tsp sugar
Shake with ice and strain into
a large glass about ⅓ full of
crushed ice. Decorate with a
cherry speared to a wedge of
fruit, preferably fresh
pineapple. Serve with a small
straw.

Trinidad Rum Cocktail

1½ oz rum
2 dashes Angostura bitters
Sugar to taste
Crushed ice
Shake together really well and
strain into a glass.

Pineapple Cocktail

1½ oz rum
¾ oz pineapple juice
½ tsp lemon juice
Shake with ice and strain into
a cocktail glass.

Rum Sour

2 oz rum
½ tsp sugar
Juice of ½ lemon
Shake with ice and strain into
a glass. Garnish with half a
slice of lemon and a cherry.

Spanish Town Cocktail

2 oz rum
1 tsp Triple Sec
Stir with ice and strain into
cocktail glasses.

Yellow Bird

1½ oz rum
3 oz pineapple juice
¼ oz orange juice
¾ oz Creme de Banana
Dash of Galliano
¼ oz Apricot Brandy
Shake well and serve in a tall
glass.

Bossa Nova

4 parts dark rum
1 part lime juice
1 part lemon juice
2 parts passion fruit juice
Shake well and strain into a
medium-sized glass. Serve
with crushed ice and decorate
with slices of orange and lime.

13

Rumba

2 parts dark rum
1 part light rum
1 part lime juice

1 part gin
1 part lemon juice
2 dashes Grenadine

Shake well and strain into a tall glass. Top up with soda water
and serve with slices of lemon and lime.

Rum Nog

1 measure dark rum
1 level tsp sugar
Nutmeg to taste

1 egg
1 glass milk

Shake vigorously and strain into a tall glass. Serve with a
sprinkling of nutmeg.

Fruit & Rum

The sweet and sometimes sour taste of Caribbean fruits mixes particularly well with the richness of rum.

Pineapple Caribbean

1 pineapple	½ oz cherry brandy
3 cubes ice	1 dash Angostura bitters
1 oz vodka	12 Maraschino cherries
1 oz Cockspur dark rum	Lemon slices
½ oz apricot brandy	1 olive

Slice top off pineapple about 2" from top. Hollow out the pineapple and cut half the fruit into small cubes. Place fruit back in pineapple. Into cocktail shaker put ice cubes, vodka, rum, apricot brandy, cherry brandy and bitters and shake. Pour unstrained over the fruit in the pineapple shell. Place 4 toothpicks around the edge of the pineapple shell and thread 3 cherries on to each toothpick. Place 4 toothpicks in lid of pineapple to correspond with position of bottom toothpicks. Place lid back so that toothpicks go into the cherries. Decorate with 2 slices (round) of lemon, ¼" thick, one slice on either side of pineapple. Balance two crossed swizzle sticks on toothpick that goes through the lemon. Secure the sticks by placing an olive on the exposed part of the toothpick. Serve with a spoon and drinking straws.

Rum Daisy

⅓ glass white rum
Juice of ½ lemon
1 tbsp Grenadine
Cherries
Bananas
Shake the liquid ingredients together and decorate with cherries and bananas.

Highballs

Traditionally, highballs are the most thirst quenching drinks served in a tall glass with plenty of ice.

Rum Screwdriver

1½ oz Cockspur rum
Orange juice
Ice cubes
Pour the orange juice over the
ice cubes and top with the
rum measure.

Rum Highball

1½ oz rum
Ice cubes
Ginger ale
Put all the ingredients into a
tall glass and garnish with zest
of lemon or orange.

Durkee Highball-soda

1½ oz rum
1 tbsp Triple Sec
1 tsp sugar syrup
Soda water
Ice cubes
Shake the rum, Triple Sec and
sugar syrup together
thoroughly with ice. Strain into
a glass and top up with soda
water.

Rum Rickey

1½ oz rum
Juice of ½ lime
Soda water
Pour the lime juice into a tall
glass containing ice cubes, add
the rum and top up with soda
water.

Rum Collins

1½ oz rum
2 tsp sugar
Juice of 1 lemon
Fizzy orangeade
Ice cubes
Dash of Angostura bitters
Pour all the ingredients into a
tall glass, garnish with a slice
of orange, a cherry and a
piece of banana.

Juleps

There are many julep recipes – most of them include plenty of crushed ice and a generous garnish of mint sprigs and fresh fruit.

Rum Julep

1½ oz rum
3 sprigs mint
1 tsp sugar
1 tbsp water
Lightly crush the mint with the sugar and water. Add rum and garnish with mint leaves.

Rum Mojito
The famous Cuban drink

2 oz white rum
¼ oz lemon juice
1 tsp sugar
Several ice cubes
Soda water
2 drops Angostura bitters
Mint leaves
Stir sugar and lemon juice well, add the rum and ice. Top the glass up with soda water, add bitters and garnish with mint leaves.

Trinidad Swizzle

1 oz dark rum
1 oz amber rum
1 oz Grand Marnier
¼ oz lime juice
2 dashes Grenadine syrup
½ oz mango juice
Sugar cane stick
Cherry
Sprig of mint
Slice of orange
Shake all the liquids with the crushed ice, pour into a tall glass. Add more crushed ice and garnish with the cherry, mint and slice of orange.

Pina Colada

Possibly one of the most famous Caribbean rum drinks.

Pina Colada
is a classic

1½ oz rum
1 oz cream of coconut
3 oz unsweetened pineapple juice
1 cup crushed ice
Combine all the ingredients in a blender for 10 to 20 seconds.
Serve in a tall glass, with a straw, and garnish with pineapple.

Punches

Another popular family of drinks. A good rum punch should be a subtle blend of flavours, well mixed and attractively presented.

Bishop's Punch

4 tbsp brandy
¼ pint rum
¼ pint peach brandy
½ pint strained lime juice

12 oz sugar
2½ pints soda water

Mix brandy, rum, peach brandy and lime juice and pour onto the sugar in a bowl. When sugar has dissolved, add soda water and ice.

Champagne Punch

3 pineapples, sliced and
    crushed
2 cups lemon juice
1 lb sugar

4 bottles Champagne
½ cup Curaçao
½ cup cherry juice
2 pints rum

Dissolve the sugar in the lemon juice and add the pineapple, Curaçao and cherry juice. Chill for 2 hours. Pour this mixture over ice in a bowl and add 4 bottles of Champagne. Stir gently and serve immediately.

Party Punch

16 oz orange juice   16 oz rum
16 oz pineapple juice   Sugar to taste
16 oz Club soda   3 oz lime juice
Pour all the ingredients into a large punch bowl with crushed ice.

Planter's Punch

3 parts rum
1 part lime juice
2 parts sugar syrup
3 parts water
Dash of Curaçao or
Angostura bitters
Combine all the ingredients
and serve in tall glasses with
cherries and orange slices.

Pirates Punch

2 parts rum
1 part sweet vermouth

Dash of Angostura bitters

Shake well with ice and strain into a glass.

Carlisle Rum Punch

½ pint strained lime juice
¼ pint strained orange juice
¼ pint strained pineapple juice
2 tbsp sugar syrup
2 or 3 dashes Angostura
    bitters

Cherries
¾ pint rum
Cracked ice
Grated nutmeg
Halved pineapple slices
Orange slices

Mix all ingredients except ice and fruit in a bowl. Half fill cups with cracked ice, fill up with punch, sprinkle with nutmeg and float pineapple and orange slices and cherries on top.

Rum & One

Simple rum drinks have a clear and crisp flavour. Here are some suggestions for rum and one mixes. Why not conjure up some of your own?

Rum and Tonic

1½ oz rum poured on ice, topped with tonic water and garnished with a slice of lemon or lime.

Rum and Coke

1½ oz rum poured on ice and topped up with coke.

Teatotaller

1 part iced tea
1 part rum
Stir the tea and rum together with ice and serve in tall glasses.

Rum Gimlet

Pour 1½ oz rum over ice into a cocktail glass. Add ½ oz lime juice cordial and decorate with a slice of fresh lime.

White Rum

Drinks made with white rum are naturally mellow yet refreshing.

Virgin Islands Creme Punch

2 bottles beer
6 eggs
2½ tins condensed milk
1½ tins evaporated milk
Juice of 1 lime

½ pint white rum
3 tsp Angostura bitters
½ tsp nutmeg
1 tsp vanilla

Whip eggs with lime juice. Add rum, milk and bitters and blend well. Add beer and pour into glasses of crushed ice.

Naked Lady

1½ oz white rum
1½ oz sweet vermouth
4 dashes apricot brandy

2 dashes Grenadine
4 dashes lemon juice

Shake well with ice and strain into a cocktail glass.

Rum Martini

4–5 ice cubes
1 part dry French vermouth
3 parts white rum
1 slice fresh lemon rind
Put the ice cubes into a glass
jug, pour the vermouth and
rum over the ice. Stir
vigorously, strain into a chilled
Martini glass. Twist the fresh
lemon rind over the drink and
drop it in.

Rum Bloody Mary

1½ oz white rum
4–5 oz tomato juice
Squeeze of fresh lemon
Dash of Tabasco sauce
Dash of Worcester sauce
Shake well and strain into a
`wineglass. Add salt and freshly
ground black pepper to taste.

Hot Rum

The smooth and soothing taste of these hot rum recipes will warm you during the cooler winter evenings.

Hot Punch

1 tbsp powdered ginger
3 pints (U.S. 7½ cups)
    warmed beer
3 eggs

Scant ¼ pint (U.S. ½ cup) rum
1 tsp grated nutmeg
2 tbsp molasses

Blend the ginger and nutmeg with 2½ pints (U.S. 6¾ cups) beer and heat. Beat the eggs with the remaining beer and molasses. Add the warm beer to the egg mixture a little at a time, beating all the time. Add the rum and serve at once.

Hot Rum Toddy

Put 2 oz rum in a mug with one tsp sugar and add 3 oz of hot water and stir well. Add a twist of lemon or orange peel.

Cafe Calypso (Hot)

4 cups freshly percolated coffee
8 tbsp Cockspur dark rum
12 tbsp Rumona
¼ pint whipped cream

Blend the Rumona and rum gently with the coffee in a heat-proof jug. The coffee should be hot but not boiling. Serve the drink in large coffee cups, sweetened slightly with castor sugar and topped with whipped cream.

Special Hot Jamaican Rum Punch

1 bottle rum	1 bottle brandy
2 lemons	½ bottle sherry
4 oz sugar	1 tsp ginger
Up to 3½ pints boiling water	Grated nutmeg

Grate the rind of the lemons into a small earthenware bowl and add sugar. Macerate sugar and lemon gratings, add the juice of lemons and ginger. Mix well and place in another large earthenware bowl previously heated. Then add, in the following order, rum, brandy, sherry and boiling water. Mix well, sweeten further if desired and stand near heat for 20 minutes before serving in glasses or mugs with a grating of nutmeg on top.

Hot Rum and Chocolate

Add 2 oz rum to a cup of hot chocolate and top with whipped cream.

Cooking with Rum

Cooking with rum offers many opportunities to prepare enjoyable dishes. The addition of rum provides a special quality to enhance almost any meal. It can be added to soups and the dressings for salads, to main courses such as steak and chicken, and to desserts whether mousses, souffles or cakes. A very small number of recipes are included here as examples of how rum can be used to delight the palate.

Sweet and Sour Poussins Served with Peaches and Appleton Rum Sauce

4 poussins
1 tbsp oil
2 oz butter
3 tbsp Appleton Gold Rum
1½ tbsp flour
¼ pint white wine

¾ pint chicken stock
Juice of 1 lemon
3 dstsp dark brown sugar
1-2 tbsp tomato purée
4-6 peach halves (tinned or fresh)

Heat oil in frying pan, drop in butter. Brown poussins all over in oil and butter and place in roasting tin. While still warm, heat Appleton Rum in small saucepan, pour over poussins and set alight. When flames have died down keep warm.

Make the sauce - tip remaining oil and butter from frying pan into a saucepan and stir in flour (adding a little more butter if necessary). Gradually stir in wine, stock, lemon juice, sugar and tomato purée. Bring to boil stirring constantly. Blend Appleton Rum and juices from roasting tin into sauce. Season with salt and pepper. Pour over poussins, cover with foil and place in moderate to hot oven (190°C, Gas Mark 5-6) for 40-45 minutes.

Add peaches to poussins for last 5-10 minutes. When ready, place poussins and peaches on warm serving dish. Stir sauce, incorporating any juices from poussins and pour over poussins and peaches.
Serves 4.

Chocolate Rum Mousse

1 pkt chocolate chips   2 tbsp rum
2 tbsp water   5 eggs
Melt chocolate chips over low heat. Stir in rum. Separate eggs and beat chocolate mixture into the yolks. Beat egg whites separately and fold in. Pour into custard cups and chill for at least 4 hours.
Serves 8.

Caribbean fruits in rum

2 tangerines
3 mangoes
1 lb strawberries, hulled
½ pineapple, peeled and diced

2 inch stick cinnamon
2 lb brown sugar
2 lb granulated sugar
1½ pints rum.

Peel tangerines, removing all the pith, divide into segments and discard pips. Peel mangoes, remove stones and slice. Put the fruits in a large bowl with the cinnamon stick. Add the sugars and toss the fruit. Set aside for 1 hour turning the fruit over three or four times to ensure even distribution of the sugar.

Appleton Rum Coffee Cake

8 inch ring shape cake tin or 8 inch diameter deep cake tin

4 oz butter	2 fluid oz Appleton Gold Rum
4 oz sugar	or similar Caribbean rum
2 eggs	½ pint double or whipping
1–2 drops vanilla essence	cream
4 oz self-raising flour	6 oz walnuts – chopped
Pinch of salt	coarsely
½ fluid oz cold strong black coffee	

Beat together butter and sugar until lemon coloured, light and fluffy. Very gradually beat in the eggs, beating thoroughly between each addition. Add the vanilla essence. Sieve flour and salt, and fold into the mixture. Turn into well greased cake tin and bake in moderate oven (180°C, Gas Mark 4) for 30–35 minutes.

Turn cake out of tin and allow to cool. When completely cold, turn back into tin and stab with fork or skewer at ½ inch intervals all round the cake. Pour coffee and rum over and allow to soak for at least 1–2 hours.

Whip cream until it just holds its shape. Turn cake out onto serving dish and cover with cream. Scatter with walnuts. Serves 8.

Rum Gâteau

4 oz softened butter	1 oz cornflour
6 oz plain flour	½ oz cornflour
4 eggs	Zest and juice of 3 limes
8 oz sugar	½ pint double cream, lightly
5 oz dark rum	whipped

Pre-heat the oven to a moderate heat (190°C, Gas Mark 5-6). Butter and flour an 8 inch cake tin.

Sieve together the cornflour, flour and baking powder. Cream the butter and sugar together. Beat well until light and fluffy. Beat in the eggs one at a time, beating well all the time. Add the rum and the grated lime zest and juice. Continue beating to a smooth cream.

Fold the flour into the creamed butter and sugar mix. Pour the cake mix into the cake tin. Place in the middle of the oven for approximately one hour.

Cool the cake before removing it from the tin, then let cake cool completely on a wire rack. Cut the cake into three layers. Spread a third of the cream on each layer and sandwich together. Cover the cake with the remaining cream and decorate with whole cherries and chocolate curls.